LIFE IN A
ROMAN
TOWN

JANE SHUTER

Heinemann
LIBRARY

Customer Service   888–454–2279

Visit our website at www.heinemannlibrary.com

Produced for Heinemann Library by
    Bender Richardson White.
Photo research by Cathy Stastny and
    Maria Joannou
Designed by Ben White and
    Ron Kamen
Printed in China

09 08 07 06 05
10 9 8 7 6 5 4 3 2 1

**Library of Congress Cataloging-in-Publication
Data**

Shuter, Jane.
  Life in a Roman town / Jane Shuter.
      p. cm. -- (Picture the past)
  Includes bibliographical references and index.
  ISBN 1-4034-5828-6 (hardcover) -- ISBN 1-4034-
5836-7 (pbk.)
  1. Rome--Social life and customs--Juvenile
literature. 2. City and town life--Rome--Juvenile
literature. I. Title. II. Series.
  DG78.S49 2004
  937'009732--dc22

                                        2004002368

Acknowledgements:
The publishers would like to thank the following for
permission to reproduce photographs: Ancient
Art and Architecture/R. Sheridan pp. **9**, **10**, **14**,
17, **23**, **26**; Corbis Images Inc./Araldo de Luca
p. **22**; Jane Shuter p. **28**; John Seely pp. **8**, **16**, **18**,
19, **21**, **27**; Terry Griffiths/Magnet Harlequin p. **13**;
Trevor Clifford p. **12**; Werner Forman Archive
pp. **6**, **30**; Werner Forman Archive/Museo
Nazionale Romano, Rome p. **20**; Werner Forman
Archive/Scavi di Ostia p. **25**.

Cover photograph of a Pompeii relief showing
coppersmith's workshop reproduced with
permission of Ancient Art and Architecture/R.
Sheridan.

Every effort has been made to contact copyright
holders of any material reproduced in this book.
Any omissions will be rectified in subsequent
printings if notice is given to the publishers.

Some words are shown in bold, **like this**.
You can find out what they mean by
looking in the Glossary.

ABOUT THIS BOOK

This book is about daily life in towns in Roman times. The Romans ruled from about 753 B.C.E to 476 C.E. At first, they just ruled the city of Rome, in Italy, and the land around it. However, they formed a strong army and a built a huge **empire** by taking over more and more land and ruling it with Roman **laws**. By 265 B.C.E., they controlled most of Italy. Wherever they went, they built towns like those in Italy. The towns were important because the Romans ran the country from them.

We have illustrated this book with photographs of objects and buildings from Roman times. We have also used artists' ideas of town life. These drawings are based on Roman towns that have been found and investigated by **archaeologists**.

The author

Jane Shuter is a professional writer and editor of non-fiction books for children. She graduated from Lancaster University in 1976 with a BA honours degree and then earned a teaching qualification. She taught from 1976 to 1983, changing to editing and writing when her son was born. She lives in Oxford with her husband and son.

Contents

Roman Towns

By about 100 C.E., the Roman **Empire** had spread far and wide. Wherever the Romans went, they took Roman ways with them. They built new towns in the Roman style. The streets were straight and in a criss-cross pattern. In the town center, there was an open-air meeting place, the forum. Markets were held here. Usually there was also a basilica, which was a large building that everyone used. **Officials** ran the area from here. Each town also had **public baths,** toilets, and a system of drains and piped water.

Look for these: The **arena** shows you the subject of each double-page chapter in the book. The Roman **senator** shows you boxes with interesting facts, figures, and quotes about Roman towns.

TIMELINE OF EVENTS IN THIS BOOK

753–730 B.C.E. The city of Rome is built.

509 B.C.E. The Roman army begins to capture lands around Rome.

| 750 B.C.E. | 625 B.C.E. | 500 B.C.E. | 375 B.C.E. | 250 B.C.E. |

The Roman Empire
in C.E. 117

• towns

North
Sea

York
Britain
London

Atlantic
Ocean

ASIA

Rhine River

Paris • Trier
Gaul
Germany
Danube River

Augsburg

Bordeaux
Lyons
Milan
Novi Sad
Apulum

Spain
Bologna
Split
Black Sea

Saragossa • Narbonne
Sinop

Cordoba
Tarragona
Rome
Constantinople

Naples
Apollonia
Ankara

Italy

Nusaybin

Tangir
Caesarea
Greece
Ephesus

Carthage
Syracuse
Athens
Antioch
Palmyra

Tyre

Mediterranean Sea

Leptis Magna   Cyrene
Caesarea

AFRICA
Alexandria
Petra

Memphis
Egypt

Red Sea

Nile River

0   500 miles
0   500 kilometres

This map shows the Roman Empire at its biggest, in about 117 C.E. The main towns at that time were Pompeii and Herculaneum. They are near Naples, in Italy.

241 B.C.E. The army captures land outside Italy for the first time—the island of Sicily.

41 B.C.E. The Romans make Lyon the town at the center of their road system in Gaul (what is today France).

50 C.E. The Romans begin work on their first town in England—London.

98–180 C.E. Rome is at its most powerful. Most towns are built at this time.

250 B.C.E.   125 B.C.E.   0   125 C.E.   250 C.E.

79 C.E. Pompeii and Herculaneum, in Italy, are buried by the explosion of the volcano Vesuvius.

200 C.E. From this time the Roman Empire stops growing and begins to lose control of its lands.

Who Lived Where?

A great many people lived and worked in a town. So the town was crowded and noisy, from dawn until late evening. Wealthy people lived in big houses near the edge of town, where it was a little quieter. Craftworkers, such as potters and jewelers, had shops near the forum. They usually lived above their shops. The main roads in and out of towns were lined with tombs of the wealthy.

This is just one end—the eastern end—of the forum in Rome. The building with the little dome, on the left, is a **temple.** The big arches behind it are the remains of a basilica, one of the biggest in the forum.

Every town had:
- an open-air meeting place, the forum
- offices for the **officials** who ran the area
- at least one basilica
- a temple
- **public baths**
- shops and inns.

Workers with noisy, smelly jobs—such as leather makers, butchers, and metalworkers—lived in the poorer part of town. Here, the streets were narrower, and the buildings higher. Many people lived crammed together like in crowded apartment buildings. The poorest people of all wandered the streets begging and slept in doorways at night.

Towns often had theaters with a raised stage and seats in a half-circle shape, rising up from ground level. Theatres were built near the town centre.

The Forum

The forum was an open-air space, usually in the middle of a town. It was used for meetings and markets. All around the forum were important buildings. There were **temples** to Roman gods and goddesses. There were the basilicas from which **officials** ran the country and organized what went on in the town. The officials had to make sure drains worked and the markets ran properly.

This is part of the forum of Pompeii, in Italy. The column on the far right is where the temple of Jupiter, god of the sky, stood. The paved area between that and the next set of columns had a roof to make a shady walkway.

The **law** courts were also in the basilica building. When the lawyers and officials were not using the basilica, it was used for markets or public meetings. People, mostly men, also came to the forum to talk, find work, or arrange a marriage or a business deal. Women and children, especially from rich families, mainly stayed at home. The roads into the forum were packed with people and slow, heavy carts carrying goods to be sold or traded.

Rich **senators,** like these, met in the forum to talk business. They also ruled the **empire,** until **emperors** took over, from 27 B.C.E. When they ran the empire they did all their decision-making at the forum.

The Baths

All Roman towns had **public baths.** Here people could wash, bathe, swim, and exercise. Some towns had several public baths, each with different entry charges depending on what they provided. The cheapest public baths just had a changing room and three connecting rooms, kept at different temperatures. There was a cold room with a cold pool, a warm room where bathers oiled and scraped themselves clean, and a hot room with a hot pool.

The entrance halls to baths, like this one, had rooms off to the right and left. They often were important meeting places for bathers, with a fountain and seating areas.

Romans bathed naked, and oiled and scraped themselves clean—there was no soap. More expensive public baths had **saunas**, open-air pools, and **slaves** to clean and massage the bathers. Some towns had public baths just for women and girls, or just for men and boys. Other baths were open to men, women, or families at different times of the day.

NOISY NEIGHBORS

The Roman writer Seneca lived opposite a public bath, "I hear all the groans and grunts of people exercising, or pretending to. I hear the slapping sounds of people being massaged. Then there are those who like to sing, or dive in loudly. The noise of people having their armpits plucked is awful."

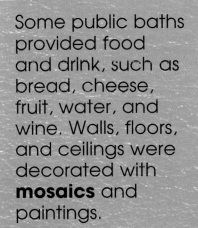

Some public baths provided food and drink, such as bread, cheese, fruit, water, and wine. Walls, floors, and ceilings were decorated with **mosaics** and paintings.

11

The Games

Most towns had a circus (an oval path for **chariot** racing) and an **arena** for games. Towns with a circus had several chariot racing teams that people supported just as people support baseball or football teams now. Each team had a different color that their drivers, horses, and supporters wore. Men, women, and children—rich and poor—all went to the circus to cheer on their teams.

The Colosseum in Rome was the biggest arena in the Roman world. It could hold 45,000 people sitting, with another 5,000 standing. On hot, sunny days there was a system of awnings to shade most of the seats.

Most shows in the arena were fights between gladiators and animals or each other. There were different teams of gladiators, each part of a different gladiator school that trained them in different ways of fighting. Sometimes, pairs of gladiators fought until one of them was killed. Many gladiators were prisoners who already were sentenced to death and could live longer—or gain their freedom—if they fought and won.

GLADIATORS

There were different kinds of gladiators:

- a *retiarius* fought with a net, to trap his opponent, and a three-pointed spear called a trident
- a *Samnite* fought with a sword and wore armor, including a helmet and a big shield
- a *Thracian* fought with a dagger, wore some body armor and carried a small, round shield.

This expensive drinking cup was decorated with a painting of gladiators. It was sent to England from Germany.

Temples

The Romans worshipped many gods and goddesses, and towns had **temples** to the most important ones. Temples were houses for statues of the gods. They held valuable presents given to the gods. Only the **priests** and **priestesses** who served the gods went into temples. Ordinary people waited just outside temples on special days, where **religious ceremonies** were held.

WHO PAID?

Temples were expensive to build. Wealthy people often had them built as a way to thank the gods for a favor. Sometimes the people who ran each town decided to build a temple. The money came from the **taxes** that everyone had to pay.

These priests are holding an open-air ceremony for the goddess Isis. She was an Egyptian goddess, but the Romans added her to their gods and goddesses when they took over Egypt.

Ordinary people worshipped at **shrines** set up in towns and in the countryside. Every home also had a small shrine, where the family worshipped the gods and goddesses who took care of the house. Roman prayers were usually a bargain with a particular god or goddess. They offered them a gift and expected the gods to do something in return.

Most temples had:
- a grand entrance, with steps, columns that held up carved stonework, and an upside-down V-shaped roof
- no windows and just one door
- an **altar** used by the priests at festival times
- statues to the gods and goddesses.

The Theater

Townspeople went to the theater often. The theater was open-air, with a stage and a seating area in the shape of a half-circle. The audience sat on stone benches that went up in steps. Women and young children had to sit separately from the men. Plays were either funny comedies or tragedies, where things turned out badly. Many plays were put on as part of **religious festivals** and **ceremonies,** and performed to please the gods.

This theater in Pompeii, Italy, held about 5,000 people. The biggest theater of all, in Rome, held 27,000. Seats were different prices—the cheapest were at the top.

All the actors in the theater were men. They wore different masks to show what kind of person they were playing. Brown masks were for men, white for women. The masks had different expressions, too. Musicians played pipes, banged drums, and shook tambourines during the play, making the music sad or happy to match what was happening on stage.

CLOTHES

The color of the clothes the actors wore also told you who they were playing. Old men wore white, and young men wore several colors together. Rich people wore purple, the poor wore red, and slaves wore very short **tunics.**

The actors in this **mosaic** are shown in their dressing room— a big space behind the stage. The actors have **slaves** to help them change, something only large theaters could afford.

Homes

In towns, most family homes were built two stories high, with rooms facing inwards to an **atrium** or courtyard. The atrium was open to the sky, often with a pool in the middle to catch rainwater and a covered walkway all around it at ground level. The rooms on the ground floor opened onto the atrium. Craftworkers' homes had a shop open to the street, so passersby could buy the things they made.

Wealthy people often had a garden at the back of their town house, like this one. The garden had a **porch** running all around it to give shade in summer and shelter from the rain in winter.

Poorer townspeople lived in two- or three-story buildings called *insulae*, like apartment buildings. A whole family sometimes shared one room. They lived, ate, cooked on a fire, and slept in the room. Most *insulae* did not have toilets or piped water. They were badly built. Because they were crammed with people and had wooden beams and floors, there was a danger of fire. The poorer areas of towns burned down often.

FALLING DOWN

The Roman writer Juvenal was talking about the *insulae* of Rome when he said, "Most of the city is propped up with planks of wood to stop it from falling down. The landlord says 'sleep well' when he knows you will be lucky if the building stays up through the night."

Homes like this one, that had walls on the street, often had only small windows with metal bars set in them on the street side. This was to keep the houses safe from burglars.

19

Work

In Roman times, women ran the home. They shopped, cooked, and raised their children, or had **slaves** to do this for them. Men went out to work. Wealthy men did not work, but left the house to do different kinds of business, such as buying and selling slaves. Craftworkers had workshops, and sold **goods** from there or at markets in the forum. Traders had offices near the docks, where there were also warehouses to store the goods they bought and sold.

This carving shows a shoemaker and his assistant in their workshop. The shoemaker kept a few sizes of the types of shoe he made in a cupboard. People chose a style from his stock, then he measured their feet and made the shoes to fit exactly.

WOMEN AT WORK

Married women from wealthy families spent their time entertaining or making sure slaves ran the home properly. Those from poor families had to work, helping their husbands. If their husbands died, women sometimes took over and ran their businesses.

Towns were so full of shoppers that poorer people could sell things without owning a shop. They sold fruit, vegetables, and cooked food—including cakes and sausages—from stalls on the streets, or even from baskets on their heads! Other poor people worked for builders or traders, carrying heavy loads, storing goods, or mixing cement. They also worked in the inns and eating places, as cooks, cleaners, or waiters.

Some people, like the musicians and actors in this **mosaic,** made a living performing in the streets. After a performance, they collected money from people who had stopped to watch their show.

Schools

Children did not have to go to school in Roman times, but some did. There was no free education and no school buildings. Good teachers charged high fees and hired a room to teach in, often in the basilica. Other teachers charged less, but could not afford to hire a room. They taught in courtyards or shop doorways. Their classrooms were open to the street and were noisy. Some were even on the sidewalk.

SCHOOL TIME

Every day was a school day, except for a break of eight days in the summer. Lessons started at dawn and went on until midday. There was a lunch break, then school began again until about 3 P.M.

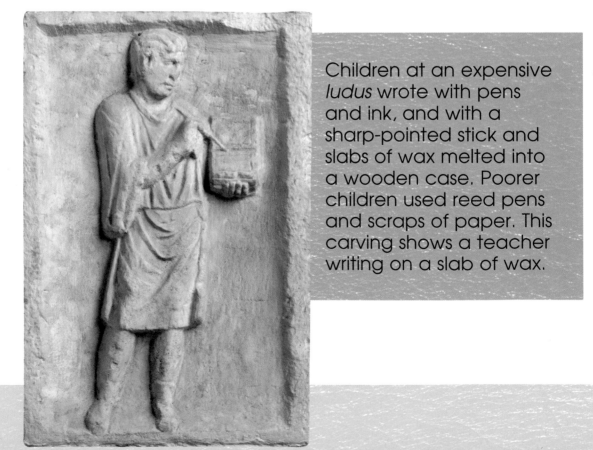

Children at an expensive *ludus* wrote with pens and ink, and with a sharp-pointed stick and slabs of wax melted into a wooden case. Poorer children used reed pens and scraps of paper. This carving shows a teacher writing on a slab of wax.

There were two kinds of school: the *ludus*, for girls and boys age seven to ten, and the *grammaticus*, for boys age eleven to fifteen. Only boys from wealthy families went to a *grammaticus*. They learned long sections of Roman and Greek writings by heart. Some wealthy parents hired a **tutor** to teach their children at home. These children might also learn music and art.

The sons of craftworkers sometimes went to a *ludus*, but then they left school and learned a trade (a specific job), like the metalworkers' sons seen here. When girls left school, they helped their mothers at home.

Clothes

Poor townspeople made their own clothes, spinning wool and weaving it into cloth. People with money to spare could buy cloth already made from weaving shops. For colored cloth, they went to dyeshops. Cloth was dyed (colored) with plant material, or even crushed insects!

Roman men and women all wore a **tunic** and a strip of cloth that was wrapped around their waist and tucked between their legs. They wore layers of tunics and lengths of cloth over these, depending on how hot it was.

Slaves or the women of the house sometimes washed underwear and things that needed special care in rainwater from the **atrium**. But most things, especially sheets, were sent to a laundry. Here, washing was done in big stone baths. Some laundries had heated rooms for drying when the weather was bad.

Children wore a *bulla*, a good-luck charm, around their necks, as in this carving. They received it when they were born, and it was one of the things they gave to the gods in the **ceremony** where they became adults.

Wealthy people had the most choice of cloth and clothing. They could buy wool or linen, usually dyed in the most expensive colors. They were the only people who could afford silk brought from the East. Wealthy men often wore a toga—a half-circle of cloth draped around the body. Wealthy women had their clothes made for them by dressmakers.

Shopping

In Roman towns you could buy almost anything, from cooking pots to sandals. Shops had a room opening onto the street, with a workspace behind where the **goods** were made. If the shopkeeper did not have what the customer wanted, he made it specially. Not all shopkeepers made the things they sold. Some shops sold expensive jewelry, painted glass, and decorated pottery brought from other countries.

Roman butchers cut their meat into pieces, then sold it by weight, just like a butcher today. You can see the weighing scale to the right of the butcher in the picture.

MARKET DAY

Markets were usually held in the forum several times a week, sometimes daily. Shopkeepers sometimes had a market stall. But the market was mainly for fresh foods such as fruit, vegetables, milk, and cheese. These had to be bought daily as there were no refrigerators to keep things cold.

Townspeople were not the only people shopping in towns. People came from villages and **villas** all around to shop. They came to buy things that they could not get locally. They sometimes also came to sell things at the town markets. Towns were especially noisy and busy on market days. The streets, crowded even on normal days, were filled with carts and animals heading to and from the markets.

Shops had a wide opening, which could be closed with a wooden shutter, and a door. Goods were usually placed on a table and hanging from hooks above it. The **porch** sheltered the customers and the goods.

Eating Out

Most wealthy Romans ate at home, or at the homes of their friends. They ate mostly meat and fish stews, cooked over an open fire. They dined out when they were traveling, in inns or taverns where they hired a room to themselves. The men snacked or drank in town bars. Most eating places sold cheap food to travelers or people who had no kitchens to cook in. The food included olives, sausages, chicken wings, bread, and cheese.

Food shops were often on street corners, like this one. This gave them two counters facing the street. Food and drink was kept warm or cool in pottery containers (bottom left), set into the counter, and sold by the bowl or glass. Customers stood at the counter.

A Roman recipe—fish sauce

The Romans used this fish sauce the way many people use tomato paste now. They put a spoonful of it in almost anything they were cooking. They also spread it on warm toast as a snack or a starter before a meal.

WARNING: Ask an adult to help you with the cooking.

You will need:
1/3 cup of unsalted anchovies or sardines, canned in olive oil
1 tablespoon vinegar
1 teapoon olive oil
1 clove of garlic, crushed
1/2 teaspoon pepper
1 teaspoon dried mixed herbs
a clean, dry glass jar with a lid.

1 Open the can of fish and put it, with the oil, into a mixing bowl.

2 Mash up the fish with a fork until it is mushy.

3 Add the garlic and mash up again until it is mixed well.

4 Add the vinegar, pepper, and herbs and stir gently until it is all mixed in.

5 Spoon the mixture into the jar and leave in the fridge for two days.

Roman Towns Now

Some modern towns, such as London (in England), Rome (in Italy) and Lyons (in France) have been lived in ever since Roman times. Some still have buildings from Roman times, such as the Colosseum in Rome. Some Roman towns are not used now, but have survived for us to visit. Of these, the most famous and best preserved are Pompeii and Herculaneum in southern Italy, buried by the eruption of a volcano in 79 C.E.

Pompeii—shown here—and Herculaneum were kept safe under the ash from the volcano. From the 1750s, people have **excavated** the towns. Ever since they have been open to the weather and weeds, preserving them has been a problem.

Glossary

altar table used during worship services

archaeologist person who uncovers old buildings and burial sites to find out about the past

arena place used for public entertainment

atrium courtyard, open space within a house

chariot platform on wheels, pulled by horses

emperor ruler of ancient Rome

empire country and all the other lands it controls

excavate dig out and remove items from the ground

goods things that are made, bought, and sold

law rule made by the people running a country

mosaic picture made up of many different colored pieces of stone fixed together

official person who helps run a country

porch roofed area that gives shelter on the outside wall of a house

priest/priestess man/woman who works in a temple, serving a god or goddess

public bath town bath that everyone can use

religious ceremony/festival special time when people go to one place to pray to the gods and goddesses

sauna room in which water is poured on hot stones to make steam

senator important and wealthy man in the Roman Empire

shrine place where people come to pray to gods and goddesses and leave them gifts

slave person who is bought and sold like property

tax money that people living in a country pay to help run the country

temple place where people pray to gods and goddesses

tunic T-shirt shaped piece of clothing that comes down to about the knees. Roman men, women, and children all wore tunics

tutor private teacher

villa large house in the country or by the sea

More Books to Read

James, Simon. *See Through History: Ancient Rome*. Chicago: Heinemann Library, 1996.

Reid, Struan. *The Life and World of Julius Caesar*. Chicago: Heinemann Library, 2002.

Seely, John and Elizabeth. *Visiting the Past: Pompeii and Herculaneum*. Chicago: Heinemann Library, 1999.

Williams, Brenda. *History of Britain: Roman Britain*. Chicago: Heinemann Library, 1997.

Index